The Music Scene

Performing Live

Matt Anniss

FRANKLIN WATTS
LONDON • SYDNEY

This edition published 2015 by
Franklin Watts
338 Euston Road
London NW1 3BH

Franklin Watts Australia
Level 17/207 Kent Street
Sydney, NSW 2000

Produced by Calcium, www.calciumcreative.co.uk

A CIP catalogue record for this book is available from
the British Library.

ISBN 978 1 4451 3941 8

Dewey classification: 781.6'4143

Printed in China

Franklin Watts is a division of Hachette Children's Books,
an Hachette UK company
www.hachette.co.uk

Acknowledgements:
The publisher would like to thank the following for permission to
reproduce photographs: Dreamstime: Ahmet Ihsan Ariturk 26–27,
Dario Diament 43t, Dragos Daniel Iliescu 27cr, Imagecollect 31bl, Pavel
Losevsky 9br, Michael Lunceford 19br, Nordjordet 28bl, Prestong 40tr,
Valentino Visentini 32bl; Istock: Anthony Brown 24cr, Steve Debenport
31tr; Lollapalozza.com: Cambria Harkey 23b; Rex Features: 38tr, James
Fortune 12bl, Adrian Sherratt 25tr, Richard Young 39br; Shutterstock:
Arvzdix 35tr, 41bl, Auremar 30tr, Carl Bjorklund 17tl, Maxim Blinkov
17cr, ChinellatoPhoto 41tr, Dfree 16bc, Andreas Gradin 6tr, Alan
Heartfield 22tr, Gynnis Jones 18tr, Konstantynov cover, Aija Lehtonen
34bl, R. Gino Santa Maria 15b, Olly 14tr, Losevsky Pavel 42bl, Kristina
Postnikova 10bl, Lev Radin 9tl, 21tr, Nikola Spasenoski 7b, 22bl, Ronald
Sumners 10tr, TDC Photography 29br, Valeria73 5br, 36–37; Wikipedia:
John Stephen Dwyer 33tl, Magnushk 14bl, Rich Niewiroski Jr 36bl,
Hilary Perkins 8bl, Kenny Sun 20b, Tabercil 11cr.

Every attempt has been made to clear copyright. Should there be any
inadvertent omission please apply to the publisher for rectification.

CONTENTS

GOING LIVE!

In a vast arena, a crowd of thousands waits. Clutching glossy tour programmes, they look out for the arrival of their musical heroes. A sudden flash of light greets tonight's entertainment, one of the best live acts in the world. With a drum roll and a flick of a guitarist's wrist, the show begins. A deafening roar of appreciation rolls round the arena.

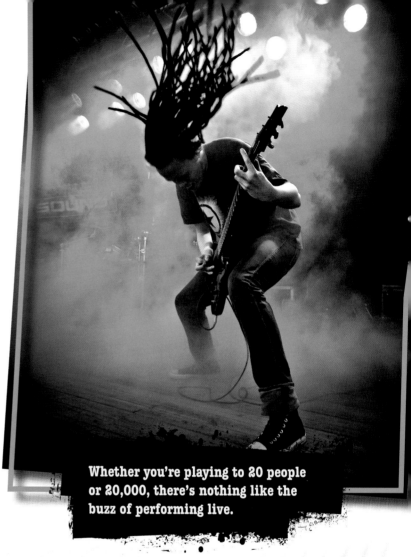

Whether you're playing to 20 people or 20,000, there's nothing like the buzz of performing live.

Just another gig

For some in the crowd, this will be a once in a lifetime event – a rare chance to see their favourite band perform their hit songs. For the band involved, it is likely to be one date on a long tour that could take them to all four corners of the globe.

Right here, right now

Live music events happen every day around the world. In fact, there will be a 'gig' happening somewhere right now. It might be a legendary rock band playing in a sports stadium, but it's just as likely to be a group of local amateurs playing to a handful of people in a bar.

Addictive feeling

Anyone who has ever performed live music will tell you what a great buzz it is. Seeing and hearing a crowd respond to a song or solo performance is hugely addictive. Being part of a musical group, be it a rock band, hip-hop crew or classical orchestra, has the feel-good factor. If you hit the right notes, everyone feels great.

The goss

Concerts and live performances are a big money-spinner for the music industry. In recent years, the live music scene has grown rapidly. In 2006, worldwide ticket sales were worth a staggering US$16.6 billion. By 2011, this had topped US$25 billion.

Love of live

For many people, it is this good feeling that makes performing live so appealing. While the best live performers can earn millions of dollars, most musicians will barely earn enough to live. Many others won't earn a penny from their performances, but continue to play gigs every weekend just for the fun of it.

Huge industry

It is not just performers who can make a living out of live music. The concert industry provides work for many hundreds of thousands, even millions, of people worldwide.

Band managers, concert promoters, sound technicians, instrument makers, costume makers, lighting specialists, security staff and bus drivers are all part of the live music industry.

When people go to see their favourite bands play live, there's a huge amount of anticipation – something that musicians can feed off to help them put on a great performance.

GOING SOLO

Anyone with some musical talent can perform live. You don't need to be the best singer in the world or the best musician, you just need to know enough chords, riffs or solos to get by. Some of the world's best-known musicians started out this way, playing low-key gigs.

Busker beginnings

One popular way for solo performers to get experience is to go out 'busking'. This is when people play on street corners or in subway stations, performing short sets of songs or instrumentals to passing members of the public. Buskers can be found in many towns and cities, showcasing their talents. If people like what they hear, they sometimes donate loose change to the musician as a way of showing their appreciation.

The road to stardom

Many famous singers and musicians have started their musical careers as weekend buskers. British singer-songwriter James Morrison first performed as a busker in Cornwall as a teenager, while Canadian rock band Barenaked Ladies busked for years before being offered their first recording contract.

Like many musicians, James Morrison had to work hard for stardom, working his way up from singing on the streets to headlining massive music festivals.

Open mic

Another good way for solo performers to get started is to get a spot at an 'open mic night'. These are concerts held at small venues designed to showcase new and inexperienced musicians. Anyone can sign up and do a 10- or 15-minute live performance, regardless of whether they've ever played live before.

On the up

Many small venues will have a designated open mic night every week. There's no limit to how many times you can perform, so many musicians return to the same venue on a regular basis. If they impress the audience, the venue manager might book them to play a small concert on their own.

The goss

British singer-songwriter Ed Sheeran started writing songs when he was 11. He left home when he was 16 and spent the next few years playing at hundreds of small venues before a live recording on YouTube caught many people's attention. By 2014, aged just 23, he had become a multi-millionaire.

Step it up

After gaining experience on the open mic circuit, good solo performers may start to pick up bookings to play at other venues in their town. If they're good enough, they may even get asked to play elsewhere in their country, or at music festivals.

Playing at small open mic nights is one way to gain experience of performing in front of an audience.

BAND PERFORMERS

Not everyone wants to perform alone. For many people, being in a band offers a more attractive route into live performance. You still get to play music live, but you're with a group of friends. You share the highs and lows, making it a less lonely experience.

Having a good chemistry between different performers is vital to the success of any band.

Band basics

Because a band is a group of musicians, there's room for people who play different instruments. For a band to be successful, everyone has to play their part. The ability to make different voices and instruments sound great together is what separates the best bands from those who will never 'make it'.

Fighting it out

Ambitious bands that write their own music have to follow a similar path to solo performers. Many get their first break at 'battle of the bands' style competitions, which are the band equivalent of open mic nights. If they impress and win the competition, they will usually be offered other performance slots at the same venue.

Many bands have enjoyed international success after being spotted playing at local 'battle of the bands' style competitions.

10

On tour

After conquering their local scene, many bands will start to pick up bookings outside their town. They might even get enough bookings to go on tour – a series of concerts around the country.

To save money, many bands will drive from gig to gig in a van, taking their equipment with them. Some will even sleep in the van!

Stagecraft

Many musicians see the long slog on their local music scene as serving an apprenticeship. It can take years of playing small, local venues for a band to build up a loyal following. Playing this many gigs allows bands to improve their performance skills (sometimes referred to as 'stagecraft') before hopefully playing bigger and better venues later in their careers. By the time they become better known, they will have learnt how to please audiences. Their musical skills will also be razor-sharp.

The goss

In 2011, a Canadian boogie-rock band called The Sheepdogs (above) won an international battle of the bands competition with a twist. Readers of famous US music magazine Rolling Stone were asked to give an unknown band a break in their 'Choose the Cover Contest'. The Sheepdogs' prize included a contract with Atlantic Records as well as the chance to be the first unsigned band ever to grace the magazine's front cover.

INDUSTRY CASE STUDY

The Rolling Stones

Very few bands have played as many concerts as rock icons The Rolling Stones. Since first performing live in London in 1962, the group has been on more than 40 concert tours. Today, they continue to perform live, 50 years after first taking to the stage.

Although they have sold loads of records, CDs and downloads, The Rolling Stones became millionaires on the back of their reputation as one of the most exciting live bands on the planet.

Club beginnings

The Rolling Stones had to work hard to achieve fame and worldwide success. Early in their career, they were given a weekly residency at a London venue called The Crawdaddy Club where they developed their skills and built up a strong fan base.

Tour tales

The Rolling Stones went on their first tour of the UK in the autumn of 1963. In the following two years, they toured the UK five more times, playing nearly 150 concerts. This relentless schedule helped them to become one of the most entertaining bands on the planet.

Live and loving it

By the 1970s, The Rolling Stones had sold enough records and played enough concerts to retire as multimillionaires. However, they enjoyed playing live so much that they continued to play concerts all over the world.

50th anniversary

In 2012 the Rolling Stones celebrated their fiftieth anniversary and played several anniversary concerts in their '50 & Counting'

Deadly gig

In 1969, a Rolling Stones' gig at the Altamont Raceway in northern California had to be stopped because of rioting and fights between concertgoers and members of a local Hells Angels motorcycle group. One person died and many others were injured. Footage of the riots and the abandoned concert was included in a film about the band called *Gimme Shelter*.

tour. The following year they played many more concerts in the USA and Europe and released a live album, *Hyde Park Live*, in the summer of 2013.

For the love of music

Every member of The Rolling Stones is a multimillionaire. Although they can earn huge sums of money from concert tours, they do not need the cash. They tour because they enjoy performing live to large crowds. Now in their 60s and 70s, their appetite for playing is as great as ever.

TIMELINE: The Rolling Stones

1962: Play their first ever concert at The Marquee Club, London

1964: Tour the USA for the first time

1969: Fan dies at the Altamont Free Concert, causing the gig to be abandoned

1972: A Rolling Stones concert at the Los Angeles Forum raises more than US$200,000 for charity

1989: End their *Steel Wheels* tour with ten dates at the Tokyo Dome

2006: Become the first British band to play the Super Bowl half-time show

2007: Play the Isle of Wight Festival, their first performance at a music festival for more than 30 years

2012/2013: Celebrate their 50th anniversary with a series of concerts

THE PROFESSIONALS

There's more to live music than fashionable bands, pop stars and solo performers. There's another group of musicians who often go unmentioned, but without whose contribution the scene would not exist. These are the professionals.

Session musicians

Professional musicians exist in many different areas of the music scene. Some, known as session musicians, can be hired by pop and rock performers to make up their backing band for concert tours and festival appearances. Session musicians are often very talented. Because they are not attached to one band or artist, they have to be able to play well in many musical styles.

Top session drummers are in high demand and can make a very good living out of playing for a number of different bands.

Solid career

Being a session musician is a solid career choice. Top session musicians are in high demand and can earn significant amounts of money. Because their fortunes aren't tied to the success of a CD or concert tour, the world's best session musicians can enjoy long and successful careers. Session musician Leland Sklar has recorded tracks with artists such as Donna Summer and Robbie Williams.

Bass guitarist Leland Sklar has played as a session musician on thousands of records over the course of his 45-year career.

The long game

Over the course of the last 50 years, many session musicians and bands have shaped the history of popular music and played with famous stars. A band called MFSB was integral to the development of the disco sound, providing backing for singers and vocal groups of the 1970s and '80s, while Los Angeles-based outfit The Wrecking Crew were so influential that they were given a place in the Music Hall of Fame in 2007.

Lots of jobs

There are a number of other opportunities for professional musicians to perform. Some television shows will employ a 'house band' to perform music, while some plays, such as musicals, require a number of musicians. If you're a talented musician and want to perform live, there are lots of jobs out there.

The goss

Some session musicians find fame in their own right. After playing on stage with Amy Winehouse, The Haggis Horns were asked by Mark Ronson to play on his Version album. The CD was a worldwide success and since then, the band has toured the world in its own right, playing to packed audiences in the US and Europe.

Session musicians don't just play on records and CDs — often, they get to go out on tour as part of a solo artist's backing band.

BEAT MASTERS

Music made using traditional and electric instruments has been performed for many years. However, it's only in recent times that the technology has existed for electronically-produced music to be performed live.

Studio music

When electronic dance music first became popular in the 1980s, it was very difficult to perform. When they wrote songs, electronic musicians did not expect to have to perform them. Instead, they recorded futuristic tracks that could be released on records or CDs. These were then played in clubs by DJs.

Computer music

In the early days of hip-hop, house and techno, tracks were made using equipment that hadn't really been designed for live performance, such as drum machines, digital samplers and computers. Many people who made dance music and hip-hop weren't trained musicians. Instead, they created their songs by a process of trial and error.

Live music

In the 1990s, dance music became more popular. Fans of dance acts such as Orbital, The Chemical Brothers, The Crystal Method, Underworld, and Daft Punk expected to be able to see them perform their songs live. These bands and others rose to the challenge, using powerful new computers, synthesisers and drum machines to recreate their music at festivals and other big events.

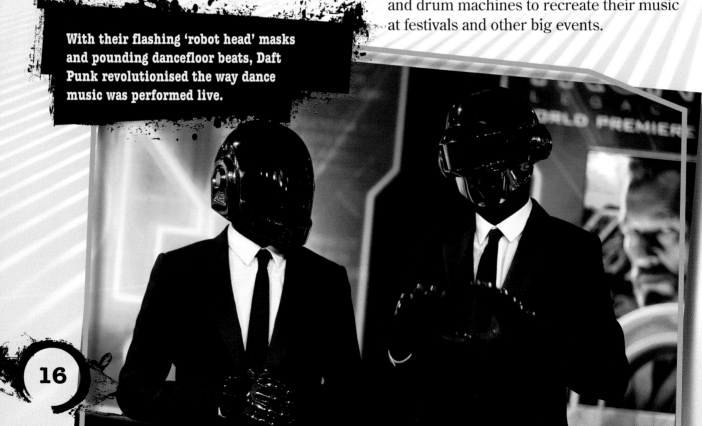

With their flashing 'robot head' masks and pounding dancefloor beats, Daft Punk revolutionised the way dance music was performed live.

The goss

One of the biggest ever dance gigs was performed by Dutch DJ Tiësto (left) in 2004. He played a short set of his own tracks at the opening ceremony of the Athens Olympics. There were 80,000 people in the stadium and hundreds of millions of people watching around the world on television.

DJs as musicians

In recent years, technology has been developed to allow DJs to turn their sets into a 'proper' live performance. Using a laptop computer and software programs such as Ableton Live or Serato Scratch Live, DJs can control every element of the tracks they play. They can change the beats, alter synthesiser loops and even replace sounds, all in real time.

In recent years, new computer software programs have blurred the boundaries between DJing and live performance.

Performance pioneer

One of the first DJs to see the potential of DJ/performance software such as Ableton Live was Ralph Lawson, the creator of 2020 Vision Recordings. He put together a band called 2020 Soundsystem in 2004. It featured three musicians performing live drums, keyboard and bass guitar.

Lawson controlled what the audience heard using his laptop and a specially designed DJ mixer. Each show was performed like a non-stop DJ set, with a blend of live songs, recorded dance tracks and electronic loops. Their first album, *No Order*, included a CD recorded live at Spain's Sonar Festival in 2006.

17

CHAPTER TWO

LIVE ON STAGE

While enormous, stadium-sized concerts from world famous rock and pop stars make the headlines, most live music is performed in small venues. Every town and city in the world has its own live music scene. These local scenes are at the heart of the live music industry.

What's on?

Take a look at the entertainment listings pages of your local newspaper, and you should find a list of gigs and concerts happening in your town. Unless you live in a tiny village, it's likely that you'll find a long list of events, many at venues you've never heard of.

Thriving local music scenes are the lifeblood of the live performance scene – without them, many musicians would never get their 'big break'.

Lots of venues

In the UK alone, there are nearly 85,000 places where you can go and watch live music on a regular basis. In the USA, the number is likely to be in the hundreds of thousands. Although some of these are dedicated concert halls, theatres or big arenas, most are much, much smaller.

The goss

The town of Austin, Texas, holds a unique record. It has more live music venues per person than any other place in the USA. It has more than 200 venues to serve 885,000 people – that's one venue for every 4,425 people who live in the town!

Local heroes

The local live music scenes that exist in each town and city around the world operate in isolation. That means they would exist even if famous bands didn't pass through the town on one of their tours. These scenes are run by local musicians, promoters and venue owners purely to entertain people in the town.

On the up

Live music is amongst the most popular downtime activities of our times, and it's getting more popular. In 2010, money raised from concert tickets overtook money raised from CD and download sales for the very first time. More people are spending money to watch singers and bands perform live than ever before. Local music scenes such as the film and music festival SXSW in Austin, Texas, are getting stronger. Since this is where all performers take their first steps into the limelight, it's great news for anyone who dreams of playing music for a living.

Local action

For a band or singer to become successful, they must first conquer their local live music scene. Arctic Monkeys may have become famous over the Internet after posting songs on Myspace, but they already had a big fan base in their home city of Sheffield in the UK.

The band first became popular in small, city centre venues such as the Hallamshire Hotel, The Grapes, and Under The Boardwalk – tiny spaces that attracted young music fans keen on watching new and unknown bands.

Performances from artists such as Macy Gray at the SXSW festival have helped Austin, Texas, to become America's undisputed live music capital.

ON TOUR

When an artist or band has gained a reputation in their local music scene, there are two routes forward: to release some music, or go on a regional or national concert tour. This is a series of performances in a number of different towns and cities, over a short period of time.

Good to go

Most musicians with dreams of success will hire a manager, someone who can help them make it big. A manager will help them record their first songs. For those songs to sell well, the artist must promote it. Traditionally, this has meant going on a concert tour. Bands such as The Black Keys focus on tours to maintain the interest of their audience.

The first tour

Ambitious performers dream about going on their first tour. This is because tours by unknown bands are rare. If venues around the country are willing to book you, it means that they think they will be able to sell enough tickets to make them money.

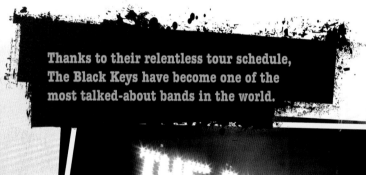

Thanks to their relentless tour schedule, The Black Keys have become one of the most talked-about bands in the world.

Tour time

Tours can vary in length enormously, depending on how well a performer is known and how much demand there is to see them play. Established bands with a successful track record may travel around the country for a month or six weeks, while new bands with just one CD to their name may only do a handful of concerts in a fortnight.

Tiring days

The life of a touring band can be relentless. After playing a concert, they may get back to their hotel well after midnight. Early the next morning, they will have to get up to travel to their next destination, which could be hundreds or thousands of kilometres away.

In demand

When they arrive at their next stop, bands have little time to rest. They set up their equipment, soundcheck (run through a few songs to make sure their instruments sound right), eat and get changed. They may also have to fit in interviews with local journalists and meet VIP guests – all within a few short hours. Once they've finished performing, the cycle begins again.

Small time

Often, a band's first concert tour will be of relatively small venues. That means they won't get paid a lot for their performances. If they want to make money from the tour, they must try to save money where they can.

The goss

Not all musicians jump at the first opportunity to tour. The Black Eyed Peas (above) are now one of the most talked about live acts on the planet, but this wasn't always the case. They originally formed in 1998, but didn't go on their first US tour until 2004.

21

FESTIVAL FEVER

Music festivals play an important role in the careers of live performers. For some, a great performance at a popular festival can put them on the music industry map. For others, a bad performance can mean the end of their career.

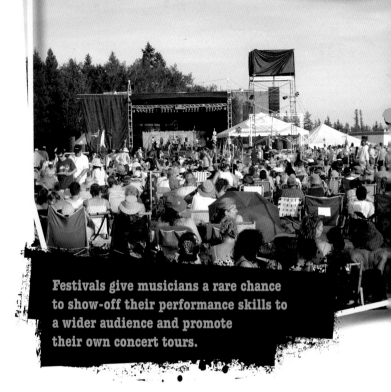

Festivals give musicians a rare chance to show-off their performance skills to a wider audience and promote their own concert tours.

Thousands in a field

Most festivals tend to take place over a long weekend, often in large parks or out in the countryside. Most festivals feature a number of stages, giving music fans a choice of bands at any one time. With anything up to ten slots on each stage every day, festivals may showcase anything between 50 and 200 bands over three or four days.

Big chance

Performers gain new fans at music festivals. Unlike their own concerts, which are usually attended by established fans, festival audiences may or may not like them, or have even heard of them before. The stakes are very high. If they perform well, they could sell more CDs or tickets to their concerts.

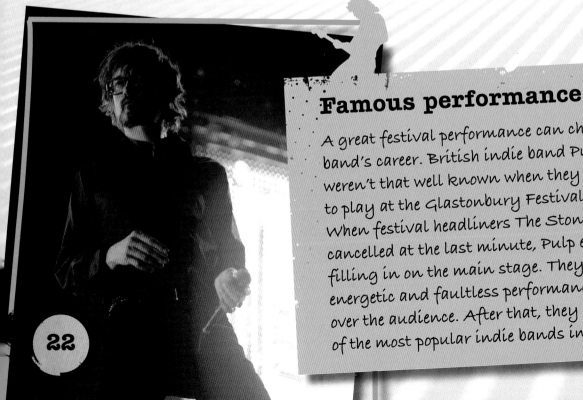

Famous performance

A great festival performance can change a band's career. British indie band Pulp (left) weren't that well known when they were booked to play at the Glastonbury Festival in 1995. When festival headliners The Stone Roses cancelled at the last minute, Pulp ended up filling in on the main stage. They put in an energetic and faultless performance, winning over the audience. After that, they became one of the most popular indie bands in the world.

Iconic appearances

Many performers have become famous for certain festival performances. Beyoncé was already well known when she headlined at Glastonbury in 2011, but footage of her dazzling performance in front of 100,000 people enhanced her reputation. American rock legend Jimi Hendrix will always be remembered for his performance at Woodstock in 1969, while Flaming Lips interrupted their 2006 show at SXSW in Texas to allow two couples to get engaged on stage. Once, Rage Against the Machine even took to the stage at Lollapalooza without any clothes on!

Missing in action

Another festival appearance that sent shockwaves around the music world took place in 2008. Rapper M.I.A. shocked fans by retiring from playing live during her set at Bonnaroo in Tennessee. She cancelled the rest of her world tour the very next day. She has since returned to the stage and continues to release albums and perform live concerts.

The goss

One of the most popular music events in the world, Lollapalooza, introduced the idea of the travelling festival. In the 1990s and 2000s, Lollapalooza would hold events in many US cities over the course of three months. Its line-up rarely changed from city to city. Now, Lollapalooza exists as a traditional festival held in one place. In 2011, it was held in Santiago, Chile, and in 2012 at Grant Park, Chicago.

Lollapalooza has become one of the world's must-attend events thanks to stunning performances from bands such as Coldplay (pictured).

Michael Eavis

Some shrewd business people have made a lot of money from music festivals. Perhaps the most famous example is British farmer Michael Eavis, who founded and still runs one of the biggest annual music events in the world: Glastonbury.

Humble origins

Michael Eavis was born in 1935 into a family of dairy farmers. In the 1950s, he inherited his father's farm in Pilton, a small village near Glastonbury in Somerset, UK. For 15 years, he worked the farm, selling his cows' milk to make a living.

Every few years, Michael Eavis takes a break. There was no Glastonbury Festival in 2012.

Inspiration

In 1969, Eavis visited the historic British city of Bath, where he stumbled across a free music festival. Called the Bath Festival of Blues, it featured performances by some of the most famous UK rock bands of the time. Excited by seeing thousands of people enjoying live music, he decided to put on a festival at his farm.

TIMELINE: Michael Eavis

1935: Born in Dorset, UK

1958: Inherits Worthy Farm in Pilton, Somerset, from his father

1969: Attends the Bath Festival of Blues

1970: Hosts the first ever Glastonbury Festival at Worthy Farm

1986: The 10th Glastonbury Festival attracts a then record crowd of 60,000

2005: A record 153,000 tickets are sold for that year's festival

2010: Glastonbury Festival celebrates its 40th birthday

2014: Michael Eavis says that the 50th festival in 2020 may be the last one

Glastonbury one

The first ever Glastonbury Festival took place on Michael Eavis' farm in June 1970. Eavis himself booked all of the bands, helped build the stage and organised the whole thing with the help of his wife Jean. Entrance cost £1 and just over 1,500 people turned up.

Building a reputation

Although early Glastonbury Festivals weren't a massive success, Eavis decided to stick with the idea. It paid off for him, as by the early 1980s more than 60,000 people would head to his farm every summer to hear some of the best bands in the world. As the years rolled by, the festival's reputation grew, and soon people were travelling from around the world to attend.

High demand

Today, the Glastonbury Festival is one of the most popular live music events in the world. Demand for tickets is so high that the event usually sells out within hours of going on sale. Between 2001 and 2012 it was produced by Festival Republic, a music events company owned by Live Nation, but has since returned to the control of the organisers.

After running the Glastonbury Festival almost single-handedly for 40 years, Michael Eavis is now assisted by his daughter Emily.

Money-spinner

The Glastonbury Festival has made Michael Eavis a lot of money. Although it is expensive to run and takes up most of Eavis' and daughter Emily's time, it is worth it. In 2013, ticket sales raised over £35 million.

Michael Eavis gives a high proportion of the profits to charity. Many of the people who work at the event are volunteers. Their wages are also donated to charity. In 2013 alone, the festival donated £2 million to good causes.

CHAPTER THREE

BEHIND THE SCENES

Although it's the performers who make their magic happen on stage, live music events would simply not exist without the dedication of people behind the scenes. From road crew, lighting specialists and sound technicians to bus drivers and tour managers, everyone has a major role to play.

Many concerts would grind to a halt without the tireless work of a lot of people behind the scenes, such as these sound technicians.

In charge

The most important member of a performer's back-room team is the tour manager. This person has a lot of responsibility. As well as making sure the artist gets to the venue on time, the tour manager also has to deal with venue owners, book hotels and sort out any problems that arise. He or she must also supervise the whole back-room team.

Join the crew

Most performers tour with a road crew. Members of the road crew are known as 'roadies'. These people do the bulk of the hard physical work.

Sorting the sound

Many rock and pop bands travel on tour with a number of specialist sound technicians. These people have an understanding of how instruments and electrical equipment work. Rock bands may employ a guitar technician, who looks after their guitars, repairs them if they break and makes sure they sound as good as they can.

Mix master

One of the most important people at a concert is the sound technician who mans the mixing desk. Every instrument and microphone is plugged into the mixing desk. It's the sound technician's job to adjust the loudness of each instrument and microphone to get the best possible sound. He or she will do this throughout the concert.

Publicity and security

On big tours, a public relations or press officer may travel with the band. It's their responsibility to handle all requests from journalists, radio stations or television companies for interviews with the band. Really famous artists may also have their own security guards. It's their job to keep the artist safe and make sure fans don't get too close.

It can take many hours for lighting technicians to set up all the special effects used in big concerts.

Lights and special effects

Some musicians like to put on a light show at their concerts. To do this, they will have a lighting technician. It's their job to test out the lights and special effects beforehand. During the show, the lighting technician will be in charge of switching the right lights on and off at set points.

The goss

Big concert tours require a lot of people behind the scenes. The programme for Lady Gaga's Monster Ball world tour listed more than 50 travelling staff members. Add in the number of uncredited roadies, riggers, set-builders and security staff, and the number of people involved in making each concert happen is likely to be nearly 100!

ROADIES

The life of a roadie isn't a glamorous one, but without their hard work and dedication, many concerts would never happen.

You and your crew

The word 'roadie' comes from the term road crew, the name given to the people behind the scenes who do all the hard physical jobs at concerts. There are no set rules for a roadie's job, and the term is often used to describe anyone who works on a tour and isn't a band member.

Many duties

First and foremost, roadies are responsible for all of the equipment a band needs to perform. That means they load and unload instruments, amplifiers and other heavy equipment from vans and trucks, take it to the stage and set it up. When the performance finishes, they go through the same process in reverse, making sure all the equipment is packed away and loaded back into vans and trucks.

Different roles

Other roadies don't haul equipment, set up lights and build the stage. They may be in charge of selling merchandise such as T-shirts and CDs to fans, or cooking food for the band and other tour staff to eat. Others may act as personal assistants to the tour manager or particular band members. Depending on the size and scale of the tour, the tasks a roadie might have to perform are wide and varied.

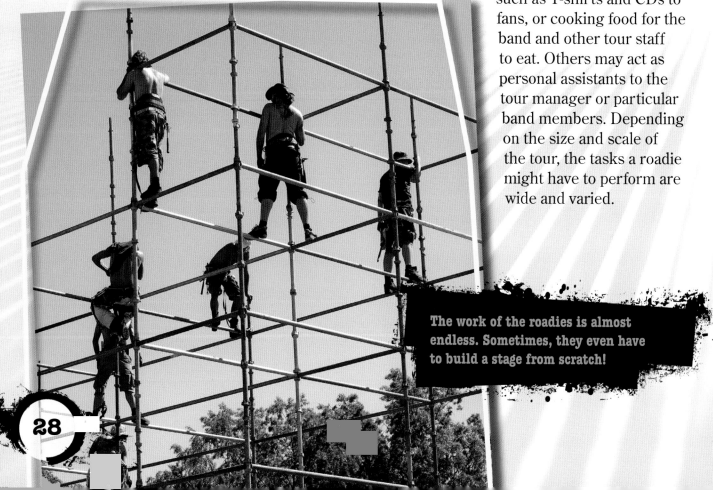

The work of the roadies is almost endless. Sometimes, they even have to build a stage from scratch!

Mobile living

In between gigs, roadies travel together, along with other tour staff, on a sleeper coach. This is a double-decker bus fitted out with bunk beds, a bathroom, a kitchen and somewhere to relax. Usually, up to 20 roadies will share one coach.

Tough break

Being a roadie is a hard job, but sometimes it can offer a way into the music business. The pay isn't great, but you get to work with a band and watch them perform. If you're an ambitious young musician, you can learn a lot from working as a roadie, not least what it takes to make a concert tour impressive and smoothly run.

The goss

It's not uncommon for roadies to fill in on stage when a band member is ill. Stuart Morgan, bass technician for U2's Adam Clayton, filled in for his boss at a concert in Sydney in 1993, while Metallica roadie John Marshall has joined the band on stage numerous times as a stand-in for James Hetfield. In 2005, Metallica's management demanded that Hetfield stop skateboarding on tour as he'd injured himself too many times!

Roadie to rock star

A number of rock stars worked as roadies before going on to worldwide musical success. Oasis guitarist Noel Gallagher worked as a roadie for early 1990s British band Inspiral Carpets, while Nirvana roadie Ben Shepherd ended up joining fellow grunge band Soundgarden.

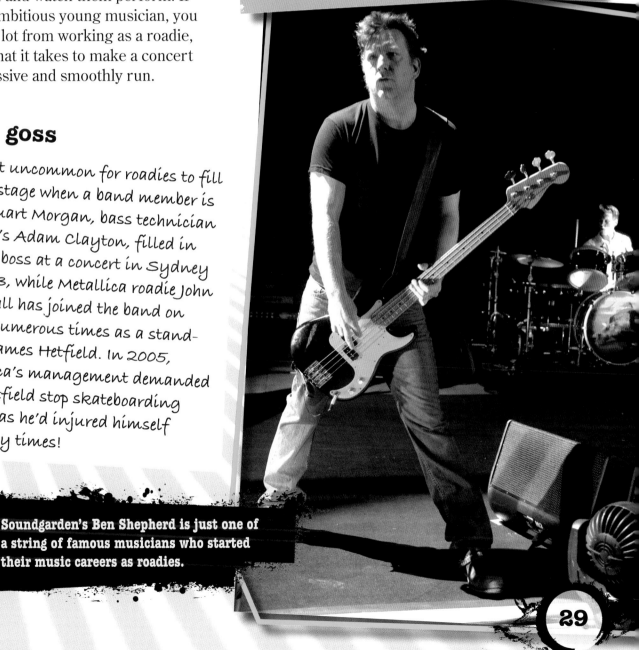

Soundgarden's Ben Shepherd is just one of a string of famous musicians who started their music careers as roadies.

GIG BUSINESS

It's not just performers who can make serious amounts of money from live music. Booking agents and concert promoters can also get very rich from concert tours.

In the book

Booking agents are the first port of call for anyone looking to put on a music event. Booking agents sign up bands they would like to represent, promising them gigs all over the country or even the world. When a performer tells their booking agent that they would like to tour, it is down to the agent to get them gigs.

Paid to get the gig

Booking agents are not always popular with venue owners and concert promoters. It's the booking agent's job to ensure that the bands they represent get good gigs that pay well. To make sure they do this, booking agents are usually paid on a commission basis. This means that a percentage of the fee paid to hire a band – usually between 10 and 20 per cent – goes directly to the agent.

Get an agent

There are very few booking agents who work solely with one band, or even on their own.

Booking agents spend a lot of time on the telephone, fielding calls from promoters keen to book the bands they represent.

The live music scene is dominated by a handful of big booking agencies. These companies employ a number of agents, each of whom represents a group of artists.

Big players

In recent years, the concert and tour promotion industry has been dominated by a small number of enormous companies. The biggest of these is US corporation Live Nation. Their competitors include the worldwide group AEG Live and UK-based companies SJM Concerts, Metropolis Music, and Mean Fiddler.

Live music for a living

Booking agents do not organise concerts. This is the job of concert promoters. They call agents to find bands to play at their events. Most concert promoters start out organising gigs in their local area, booking up bands and hiring suitable venues. They pay the band's fee and sometimes the cost of venue hire up front, gambling that they will make enough money from ticket sales to cover their costs.

Tour gamble

The next step for many concert promoters is tour promotion. This means organising a whole tour for a band. Usually, a tour promoter will agree to pay a performer's booking agent a set fee for that band to play a number of concerts. It's then down to the promoter to book the venues, promote the concerts and sell tickets.

Ticket sales are the most important thing to concert promoters – without them, they won't be able to make a living.

The goss

Concert promoters AEG lost out on millions of dollars when pop legend Michael Jackson (left) died. The company had booked the singer to play more than 30 shows at the massive O2 Arena in London, but he passed away before the shows could take place. They were forced to refund millions of ticket-holders.

KING OF POP
MICHAEL JACKSON
THIS IS IT

31

Live Nation

Live Nation is the single biggest live music events corporation in the world. Since being formed in 2005, it has grown rapidly to become one of the music industry's most dominant companies.

Clear idea

Live Nation grew out of a US company called Clear Channel Communications. Since the 1970s, Clear Channel had built up a vast empire of radio stations, outdoor advertising locations (poster sites on bus shelters and enormous roadside billboards) and concert venues. In 2005, Clear Channel's board of directors decided to transfer their concert promotion business to a new company, which they called Live Nation.

Artists on board

Owning a vast network of venues was just the beginning. In 2007, Live Nation moved to secure tour contracts for some of the world's biggest artists. Jay-Z, Madonna, U2, and Shakira all signed up to a new management company called Live Nation Artists. They all promised to play concerts exclusively for Live Nation in return for multimillion-dollar fees.

Signing up top performers such as Rihanna has helped Live Nation become one of the richest entertainment companies in the world.

RIHANNA
LOUD TOUR
JUNE 6 & 7

TICKETMASTER.CA | 1.855.985.5000

32

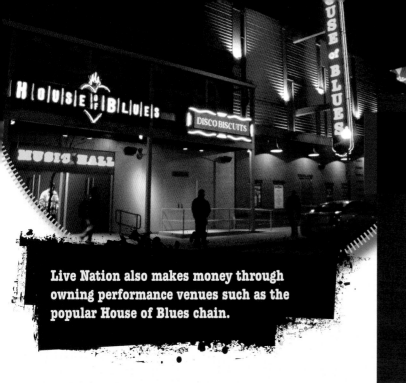

Live Nation also makes money through owning performance venues such as the popular House of Blues chain.

Other interests

Live Nation also owns a number of other companies that operate concert spaces or run music festivals. These include SFX Entertainment, which owns 135 venues around the world, and Festival Republic, the company that produces UK festivals such as Download and Latitude.

Shrewd business

The deals done with these global stars are worth far more than their recording contracts, traditionally the best money-spinners. Live Nation now effectively manages these artists, looking after all interests apart from recording contracts. They plan to launch a record label to rival the big five 'majors' of the industry.

Ticket deal

Live Nation now dominates the worldwide event ticket sales market. In 2009, it merged with the world's biggest ticketing company, Ticketmaster, to form Live Nation Entertainment. With everything under one roof, a sizeable amount of money can be earnt.

Major player

Live Nation Entertainment now dominates the live music market, both in the USA and worldwide. Every year, it promotes or produces some 22,000 concerts, selling more than US$50 million worth of tickets. Because of this and other interests, the company is now worth billions of dollars.

Unpopular

Not all music fans are keen on Live Nation. They say that the company charges too much for tickets and has a stranglehold on the live music scene. In 2012, many Madonna fans complained because tickets to see her perform cost upwards of US$150.

TIMELINE: Live Nation

1972: Clear Channel Communications forms in Los Angeles, California
2005: Live Nation forms out of Clear Channel's concert promotion business
2006: Buys the House of Blues chain of concert venues
2007: Forms Live Nation Artists and signs Madonna

2008: U2, Jay-Z, and Shakira all sign to Live Nation Artists in US$100 million deals
2009: Merges with Ticketmaster to form Live Nation Entertainment
2012: Announces major world tours from Madonna, LMFAO, Lady Gaga, and Korean pop stars BIGBANG

CHAPTER FOUR

ULTIMATE CONCERTS

When a performer becomes a household name, demand for tickets for their concerts around the world can be enormous. An ordinary tour of medium-sized venues isn't enough. To satisfy demand, artists play huge arenas, amphitheatres and stadiums.

Long haul

When an artist reaches this level of fame, nothing less than a full world tour will do. For major bands such as AC/DC, this means performing concerts worldwide over a long period of time, sometimes up to three years.

Many legs

To make life easier for the performer and road crew, long world tours are usually divided into 'legs'. Each leg will focus on a different continent or group of countries, such as North America, South America or Europe.

How long?

Just how long a tour takes depends on the number of dates in each leg, and the size of the country or continent being played. Frequently, artists on long tours may play a two-month block of dates in the USA, have a couple of weeks off, and then spend a month in Europe or touring in Japan and Australia. By the end of a two-year world tour, a performer may have played more than 100 different concerts.

Playing enormous venues allows top bands to accompany their performances with expensive pyrotechnics displays, such as this one from an AC/DC concert.

Private parties

Many of the world's top stars have a lucrative sideline performing at private parties thrown by super-rich individuals. Beyoncé (right), Usher, Mariah Carey, Elton John, and Nelly Furtado have all been paid more than US$1 million by billionaires to perform short sets at weddings, social events and secret parties.

Beyoncé is as happy playing to an invited audience of 50 or 100 as an arena full of screaming fans.

Long slog

Organising a big world tour is very hard work. Even with time off between legs, it is a tough task. On these big tours, many performers take their own sets of stages, which need to be built before the concert. Afterwards, they need to be taken down and packed away before they can be transported by road to the next gig.

Rich rewards

World tours of stadiums and huge arenas cost a great deal of money to put on. Transporting many thousands of tonnes of equipment and a large road crew around the world is not cheap. However, with anything up to 50,000 tickets being sold for each concert, it is still possible for an artist to finish their tour millions of dollars richer.

The goss

Pop legend Michael Jackson's History world tour between 1996 and 1997 is one of the most successful of all time. Jackson played 82 dates in 18 months, selling more than 4.5 million tickets! U2's worldwide 360° tour between 2009 and 2011 was the most lucrative tour of all time, making £453 million for the band. They performed 110 concerts worldwide, erecting an iconic stage and sound system wherever they went, nicknamed 'the Claw'.

U2 360 world tour

The world's most successful tour to date was the *360* tour by Irish rockers U2. Many of their previous tours, including *Zoo TV* (1992-93) and *Vertigo* (2005-06), broke attendance records. Over 3.5 million people went to concerts on the *Vertigo* tour, making it one of the ten biggest tours of all time. But for their next tour, *360*, U2 wanted to go even bigger and better.

New concept

U2 wanted the shows on their *360* tour to be spectacular. And they delivered. They asked their set designer to come up with a new concept for the stage they would perform on. He decided to make the stage round, with an enormous sound system and towering video screen positioned above it on a giant, four-legged metal claw.

Rock first

The claw-like set was the largest tour stage set ever built, stretching 51 metres high. It was incredibly complicated to set up and take apart, so three different versions were used on the tour. Each of the claw sets cost US$15 to 20 million. Between gigs, it took a fleet of 120 trucks to transport all the parts by road.

U2's record-breaking *360* tour saw the band playing to crowds of 60,000 a night.

The enormous 'claw' stage used by U2 was the most expensive ever created for a concert tour.

this high number of workers and the difficulty in assembling the stage, each concert cost around US$750,000 to put on.

Seven legs

U2 began the *360* tour in Barcelona, Spain, on 30 June 2009. By the time the tour ended in July 2011, in Moncton, Canada, the band had played 110 concerts all over the world. This included separate legs dedicated to Europe (twice), South America, Australasia, Africa and two trips to North America.

Live online

During the tour, U2 became the first band to broadcast one of their concerts live over the video-sharing website YouTube. Over 10 million people from 128 countries tuned in to watch the Rose Bowl show in Pasadena, California, on 25 October 2009.

Video stars

It wasn't just the stage itself that was complicated. The giant video screen that formed part of the claw stage set was made up of thousands of individual sections, all connected by 3,000 electrical cables.

Huge crew

The number of people required to make the tour run smoothly was enormous. There were more than 130 people in U2's travelling road crew. The band's tour promoters, Live Nation, also recruited up to 120 people to work part-time at each venue. Because of

Records tumble

Due to the enormous costs of staging the concerts, it wasn't until the latter stages of the tour that U2 began to make money. In total, U2's *360* tour took more than US$736 million in ticket sales, making it the most successful rock tour of all time. An astonishing 7.4 million people attended the 100 concerts. It was another Guinness World Record.

TIMELINE: U2

1976: Four school friends form U2 in Dublin, Ireland

1982: U2 set out on *War*, their first world tour

2005–06: Record-breaking 131-date *Vertigo* world tour begins

2009–2011: 360° worldwide tour begins in Spain and ends in Canada

2013: Their song, 'Ordinary Love' wins a Golden Globe Award

2014: *Songs of Innocence* album is given away free to iTunes users

ONE-OFF SPECTACULAR

Some of the most spectacular concerts of all time are not part of tours by individual artists, but rather big charity events featuring many different bands and artists. The most famous examples of this are Live Aid and Live 8.

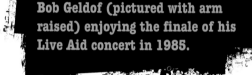

Bob Geldof (pictured with arm raised) enjoying the finale of his Live Aid concert in 1985.

Just cause

In 1984 and 1985, hundreds of thousands of people in Africa were dying of starvation. Pop stars Bob Geldof and Midge Ure wanted to do something about it, so decided to raise money to help the starving people. They put on two massive concerts on the same day in July 1985 – one at Wembley Stadium in London, UK, the other at JFK Stadium in Philadelphia in the USA.

Enormous success

Live Aid in 1985 was one of the biggest pop and rock events of all time. Millions of people around the world tuned in live on television to watch performances from artists such as Madonna, Paul McCartney, Run D.M.C., Stevie Wonder, The Rolling Stones, Bob Dylan, Queen, and Lionel Richie.

Begging calls

To make the Live Aid concerts a success, Bob Geldof and Midge Ure needed to make sure all of the world's biggest pop and rock stars were involved. They spent months phoning stars and begging them to take part. Almost all said yes.

The goss

At the Live Aid concert in Philadelphia, Rolling Stones' members Ronnie Wood and Keith Richards appeared on stage with Bob Dylan. When one of Dylan's guitar strings broke, Ronnie Wood passed him his guitar. For the rest of the performance, Wood had to make do with playing air guitar!

Millions raised

In the USA and the UK, television viewers were urged to pick up the phone and pledge whatever they could afford. Millions of people did, and the next day Bob Geldof announced that around £60 million had been raised for charity.

Playing again

In 2005, 20 years after the original Live Aid concerts, Bob Geldof decided to do it all over again. This time, the concerts would be used to persuade governments to write-off billions of dollars worth of debts owed by poor African countries. It worked, with the G8 group of the world's wealthiest countries reaching a landmark agreement at the Gleneagles summit in July 2005.

Big stars

Just like Live Aid in 1985, Live 8 featured performances from many top stars. Snoop Dogg, Green Day, The Thrills, The Killers, Scissor Sisters, Shakira, Coldplay, and Kanye West all appeared, playing sets at concerts in London, Philadelphia, Moscow, Berlin, Paris, Edinburgh, and Tokyo.

Record makers

A small number of performers appeared at both Live Aid in 1985 and Live 8 in 2005. These included U2, Madonna, Elton John, Sting, The Who, Paul McCartney, and Bob Geldof himself.

Ethiopian Birhan Woldu appeared as a starving child in a video broadcast at the 1985 Live Aid concerts. She joined Madonna on stage at Live 8 20 years later.

BEYOND THE BAND

There has always been more to live performance than just singing and playing music well. The world's best live performers are not just great musicians, but also fantastic entertainers. This is called stagecraft.

From good to great

Stagecraft is what separates good performers from great ones. If a band can play their instruments well, they will give a decent performance. Bands that put in great performances do this with flair and style, adding extra elements to make their concerts more memorable.

This giant, moving robot figure offered a spectacular stage setting for Take That's 2011 *Progress* concerts.

The goss

Sometimes, getting the audience very excited can go wrong. At the Woodstock festival in 1999, some members of the crowd started rioting and smashing things up when Limp Bizkit played their song *Break Stuff*.

Spectacular events

In the last 30 years, many performers have turned their concerts into spectacular audio-visual experiences by using elements more often found at the theatre. These include costume changes, different sets for different segments of the show, dancers, firework displays and dazzling special effects. For example, Take That's 2011 *Progress* live tour featured huge robot figures that lowered band members onto the stage, as well as towering video screens, dancers and award-winning light displays.

Trend setter

Since Madonna's pioneering tours in the 1980s, many other artists have taken a similar approach to their concerts and pulled out all the stops. Most pop artists – particularly solo performers – now surround themselves by dancers and wear many different outfits during performances.

Gaga super shows

In recent years, numerous acts have excelled at this type of musical extravaganza. The most famous is Lady Gaga, who developed a passion for stagecraft and audio-visual shows during her time working as a dancer in New York clubs. Now, her shows feature multiple costume changes, sets designed by leading artists and a troupe of more than 20 dancers. Another artist who likes to put on a spectacular show is Beyoncé.

Solo pop performers such as Lady Gaga often liven up their shows by using stunning dance routines.

Costume changes

One of the first artists to put on an entertainment spectacular was Madonna. She set a trend on her *Who's That Girl* tour in 1987 by wearing many different costumes on stage, made by some of the world's most famous fashion designers. During performances, Madonna also took part in many special dance routines. She called the show 'a musical theatre extravaganza'.

Beyoncé flies through the air on a high-wire at one of her spectacular concerts.

41

BIGGER, STRONGER, LONGER

The live music scene is in good health right now. For the first time since recorded music became popular in the 1950s, pop and rock performers are earning more money from selling concert tickets than CDs or music downloads. Live music is back.

Changing times

Traditionally, almost all bands and singers made their name on the live music circuit. By building up a following through a steady stream of concerts, they might be lucky enough to earn a recording contract.

Then, every time they made a new album they would go on tour to promote it. Playing live helped them to sell records or CDs, which is where they made the most money.

Live music revival

Now, the process has changed. Many artists still build up their reputation through live performances and then put out CDs and downloads, but now those music releases are little more than adverts for their concerts. Around the world, sales of music releases have dropped significantly because of illegal downloads, yet sales of concert tickets have been rising across the board. More people attend live music events than ever before.

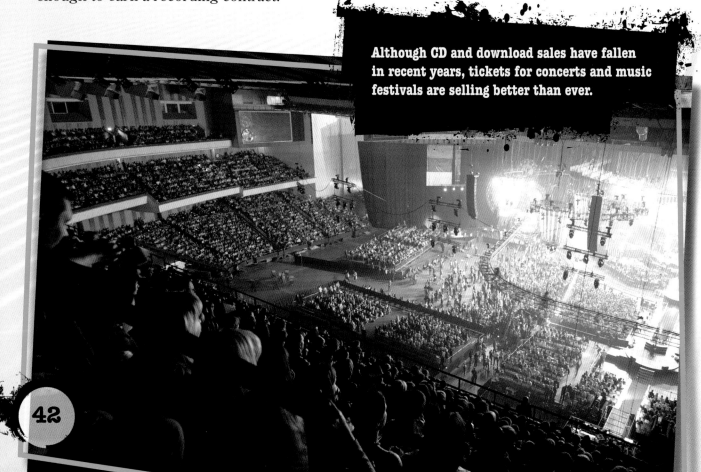

Although CD and download sales have fallen in recent years, tickets for concerts and music festivals are selling better than ever.

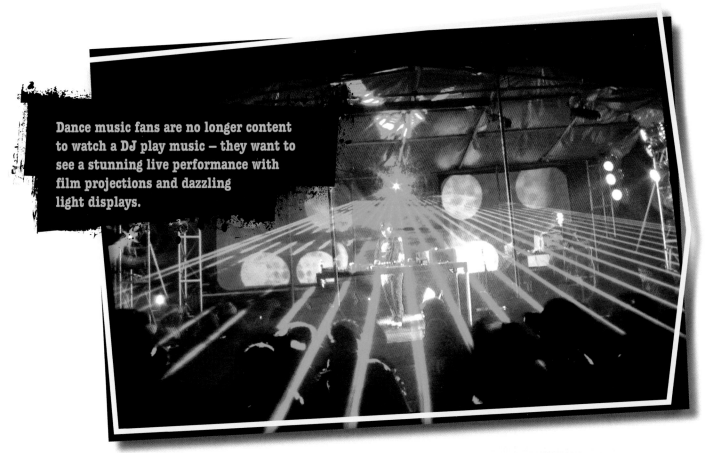

Dance music fans are no longer content to watch a DJ play music – they want to see a stunning live performance with film projections and dazzling light displays.

Big deals

It's no wonder that some musicians have decided to be managed by tour promotions companies such as the massive Live Nation group. U2, Madonna, Jay-Z, Lady Gaga, and Shakira do not need to be tied down to a record label. They can devote more of their time to touring the world, earning millions in the process. New CDs will only be released when they have a tour planned. In future, more performers may sign similar deals.

The goss

Some performers decide not to tour and instead will perform a run of shows at one big venue. Legendary singer Prince started a trend when he signed to play 21 concerts in August and September 2007 at the 20,000-capacity O2 Arena in London. Every concert sold out.

On the rise

The popularity of live events can be seen at a local level. Despite warnings from musicians that smaller venues have been closing down in recent years, figures suggest that there are now more concerts every year than ever before. Local live music scenes are getting stronger, which is good news for ambitious young bands and singers.

Dance live

Even dance and electronic artists have got on the live performance bandwagon. In the old days, dance musicians would have been content to make records and perform DJ sets. Now, more and more are developing live shows. Thanks to changes in computer technology, they can now recreate their tracks live on stage.

GLOSSARY

acoustic a term used to describe music that's made with instruments that don't need to be plugged into electric or electronic equipment

amateurs people who do something as a hobby

amphitheatres open-air concert venues, usually with seating arranged in a semi-circle facing the stage

amplifiers enormous speakers that allow the audience to hear what the band are playing

apprenticeship the process of learning a skill or trade, for example how to become a good guitarist or singer

audio-visual the combination of sound and moving images or light displays

backing band the musicians who provide the musical backing for a famous singer or rapper

band manager someone who looks after the business affairs of a musical group

busking playing music in public, for example on the street or at a train station, to try and earn a little money

chords groups of musical notes played at the same time, on a guitar or keyboard

commission being paid a wage that varies depending on how successful you are

concert promoter someone who makes a living from organising concerts

digital sampler a machine that allows you to copy small pieces of recorded music (for example a small section of a song) and alter them to make something new

electronic musicians people who make music with computers instead of conventional instruments such as Orbital

fan base people who are dedicated followers of a certain band, singer, rapper or style of music

G8 a meeting of world leaders to discuss international monetary and political affairs

gig musicians' slang for concert

headlined played the most high profile performance slot at a festival or event

high-wire a taught wire stretched high above an audience's head along which a performer 'flies' on a harness

hip-hop a type of street music that originated from the USA in the 1980s

house band a small group of musicians employed to play music in theatres or television studios

influential someone who changes the way people think or do something

instrumentals pieces of music that feature no singing or rapping

integral of vital importance

mixing desk a piece of equipment used for monitoring sound levels at a concert or in a recording studio

musicals a type of play featuring a lot of singing and dancing, usually performed in theatres

press officer the person who deals with requests from journalists for interviews with musicians

promoters people who put on and publicise concerts or club nights for a living

public relations the process of managing a person, group or business's public image and profile

R&B Rhythm and Blues

recording contract a legal agreement between a musician and a company, in which the company agrees to pay the musician to record songs and albums

44

residency when a band or artist performs regularly at a venue, usually weekly or monthly

riffs rock musicians' slang for short sequences of chords or musical melodies

riggers 'roadies' who specialise in setting up lights and stage sets

road crew also known as 'roadies', this is the collective name for all the people, bar the artist, who work on a concert tour

session musicians musicians for hire who are not attached to one particular band

soundcheck the process of testing out instruments and microphones before a performance, to make sure everything is working correctly

stagecraft a musician's performance skills, for example how they interact with an audience

synthesiser an electronic keyboard that allows users to change the way it sounds using various control buttons and dials

tour a series of concerts in different places

tour manager the person who makes sure that a concert tour runs smoothly

venues places where entertainment is performed

VIP guests VIP stands for 'very important people' – usually sponsors, friends and record label executives

FURTHER READING

Books

Martin Atkins: *Tour Smart and Break the Band* (Soluble LLC, 2007)
Pamelia S. Phillips: *Singing for Dummies* (John Wiley & Sons, 2010)
Andy Reynolds: *The Tour Book: How to Get Your Music on the Road* (Cengage, 2007)
Trev Wilkins: *Access All Areas! A Real World Guide to Gigging and Touring* (Focal Press, 2007)

Websites

Get advice about how to get your band or solo performances showcased at:
www.bbc.co.uk/programmes/profiles/24r 7mcftgLJHbN27VbKsxhJ/advice

Read top tips about perfecting your act at:
http://cheapadviceonmusic.com/

Great information and advice for musicians can be found at:
www.independentmusicadvice.com

INDEX